Chai

(खाय)

Celina Elisheba

BookLeaf Publishing

India | USA | UK

Presentation by *BookLeaf Publishing*

Web: www.bookleafpub.com

E-mail: info@bookleafpub.com

ISBN: 9789363317482

First edition 2024

I Saw Her

I saw a lonely girl,
Searching for life.
I saw her in the woods,
And gave a smile.

I saw her alone walking on the roads searching
for a friend,
Thought to accompany her
But she disappeared,
When I tried to reach her.

I saw her sitting in the room,
From the rise till the dawn.
Holding a book in her hand,
Upside down.

I tried to explain to her what life is!
But it was of no use.
As I too was not knowing it,
And gave an excuse.

I saw her alone,
I saw her incomplete.
I saw her suffocated and worried,
I saw her in the mirror.

A Journey That Ends

Walking down a hundred miles
I sit back and see my life
I can't think of much
And I just managed to smile.

People I knew
Who loved me the most
Together with whom those memories I shared
But see what an attitude, hardly I cared.

You call me fraud
You call me freak
You call me an escapist
You call me weak.

Doesn't really matter
Life is full of pain
Oh dear! So full of pain
I knew nothing I did gain.

Life went on and on
For years together
All alone
I lost and I lost it for all.

Now here I am
Beneath the clear blue sky
My people in front of me
But here I don't want to be.

I can't believe it
All I missed it
All of these words I only hear
'Rest in Peace.'

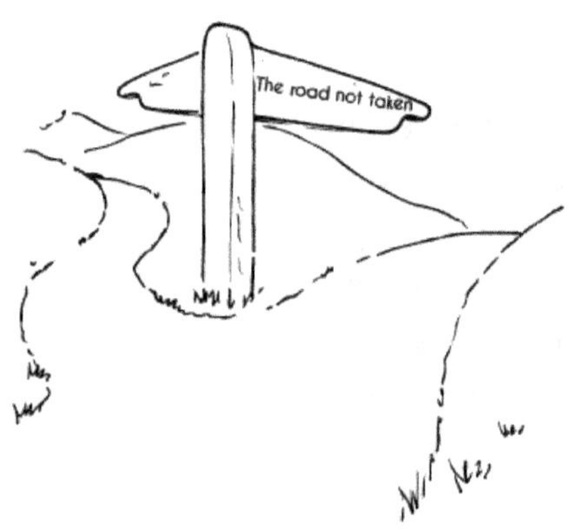

I Need A Friend

I am lost, I am lost
I don't know where
I need a friend
To get me out of there.

I don't know where to go
I am just walking with the flow
I don't want that pain
I just need a friend.

I am tired of crying
I want to smile
I want to be Me
If not forever then just for a while.

It's not easy
To read within
Just look into my eyes
They say everything

I walked on empty streets
I tried to find one on the beach
I went around places
And kept luck on guesses.

Though I found a few
Some old and some new
What else it could be
I just smiled and said
I found, I found the best in Me.

तारे भी कुछ कहते हैं

सदियों से एक तारा,
दूर आसमान से देख रहा।
वो बदलती शामें,
वो बदलती रातें,
वो बदलती इंसानों की बातें।
दूर चुपचाप सा खड़ा,
बहुत कुछ कह गया।
कई सवाल कर बैठी,
जवाब तो ना मिला
शायद कहीं
इंसानों के बोल वो सीख गया।
सुख पाता जब बादलों मे छिप जाता,
धरती की ओर, देख जो नहीं पाता।
रात भर उसे देखती रही,
सवाल करती गई, लेकिन
देखते ही देखते वो टूट गया,
क्या इसानो से वो रूठ गया?

ज़िंदगी की किताब

जिंदगी की
मेरी यह किताब।
हर पन्ने पर
बीते हुए लम्हों की याद।

साई ने दिया, कलम का साथ
जैसे दिया
तुमने मुझे तुम्हारा हाथ।

लिखती गई हर पन्ने पर तुम्हारी यादें
कितने खूबसूरत लगने लगे शब्द।
जब तुम उतर आए
हर पन्ने को रंगीन बना के।

देखो हर अक्षर
कितने रंगीन, कैसे मुस्कुराए
कलम भी शरमाई
साई को खुद मे ही पाके।

पर एक दिन ऐसा आया
साई ने छोड़ दिया कलम का साथ
और लिख ना पाई
आगे कुछ अपने आप।

सोचती हूं अब क्या करूँ
किताब पर लिखे हुए शब्द मिटा भी न पाऊँ
मेरी ज़िंदगी की किताब है वो
और मैं उन लम्हों को भुला भी न पाऊं।

बेरंग हो गए वो पन्ने
सारे अक्षर पढ़ गए धुंधले
कलम भी सूख गया
और फट गई वो ज़िंदगी की किताब।

अब कलम ने फिर से भरा नया रंग
और लिख ली अपनी नई दास्तान
नई खुशियां नए शब्द
और नई किताब।

मुस्कुराते तो वो शब्द भी हैं
कलम आज भी शर्माती है
पर यह तो ज़िंदगी की किताब है
और शायद यही ज़िंदगी है।

A Silent Road

I am left
On a silent road
People are happy
But I am unknown.
I walk quietly
To feel the air
As I smile through the way
But I don't know where.
The only noise
Comes from within, says
Speak me out, speak me out,
Helpless soul cries so loud.
It pains, it pains so much
I know
And then they say,
Just ' let go'.
I talk to the wind
I talk to these trees
I talk to these roads,
Hoping someday you meet them and get my
notes.

Give Me My Wings

Give me my wings
I want to fly.
Give me my wings
I want to touch the sky
I don't want to cry
The river of tears.
I don't want to see
The cities, full of fear.
Don't kill my hopes, set me free.
Give me my dreams
Let me be ME
I can see my existence
But let me live
I want to see this world
Let me live.

I am not weak
But I can't fight
I am not a freak
But this is not right.
Give me my wings
I want to fly
Give me my wings
I want to touch the sky.

And... I Keep Missing You...

I sit by my window,
Watching the night go.
I sit by my window,
Feeling the wind blow.

Your memories are so pure,
Shared with those tears.
Those sleepless nights,
Counted for years.

Come back! Oh! Come back,
Love me the same.
I have been alone for years,
Feeling the pain.

Show me the new world,
Show me the life there.
Take me with you,
If you really care.

I always told 'HIM'
To keep you safe, to keep you protected.
No wonder, why 'HE' kept you,
And I keep missing you…

वो नई दुनिया

इस दुनिया से निकल,
किसी और ही दुनिया में हम मिलें चल।
उस दुनिया को तुम सजाना।
रंग कहाँ भरे ये तुम बताना,
ज़माने की फ़िक्र ना हो,
लफ़्ज़ों को रोकना ना हो।
कदमों का ठहरना ना हो,
और दिलों का डरना ना हो।
कभी तुम्हारा हाथ थामूँ,
कभी तुम्हारी आंखें पढ़ूँ।
कभी तुम्हारी बातें सुनूँ,
और बस अपने दिन बिताऊँ।
किसी और का होने का एहसास जब हो,
तो वो बस तुम्हारी सांसे मुझे छू रही हो।
कुछ आहट सी जब हो,
तो वो बस तुम्हारे कदम मेरी ओर आते हों।
काश वहाँ भी बारिश हो,
काश वहाँ भी ये नीला आसमान हो।
काश उस दुनिया मे,
अपनी एक अलग ही दुनिया हो।
इस दुनिया मे हम जो न मिले,
उस दुनिया मे हम रोज़ मिलें।
इस दुनिया मे हम जो रोज़ मरे,
उस दुनिया मे हम रोज़ जियें।
तो मान लिगा,

दे ना सके तुम्हारा साथ।
इस दुनिया को कह न पाई वो बात।
ज़माने ने रोका है,
रिश्ते यहाँ निभाने हैं।
तुमसे हुए दूर,
लेकिन तुम्हारे साथ एक दुनिया हमने भी बनाई है।

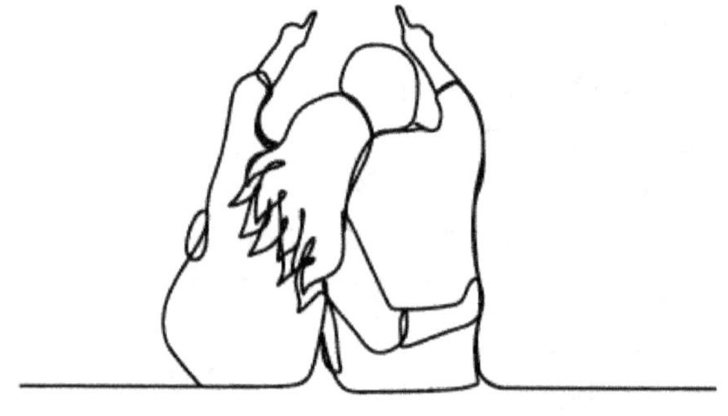

ये अधूरी कहानी

कुछ कहानियां अधूरी सी,
कुछ बातें अधूरी सी।
कुछ दिल फिर भी मिले,
कुछ लम्हें उस दिल ने जीए।

ज़रूरी नहीं कहानियां पूरी हो,
ज़रूरी नहीं बातें पूरी हो।
बस आखों में बसाकर उन्हें ,
दिल की कहानियां बयाँ हो।

ऐ ज़िंदगी ,
तेरा कोई गम नहीं।
मिलाया है दिलों को तुमने,
महलों का शौक नहीं।

कहते हैं लोग,
मतलब की है ये दुनिया।
लेकिन मेरी दुनिया को
मतलब तुमने है दिया।

लगता है कुछ खास,
जब होते हो तुम पास।
उम्मीद है रहोगे साथ,
जब चल रही हो हमारी आख़िरी सांस।

उम्मीद

ऐ ज़िंदगी तू चलती जा,
गुज़रते हुए लम्हों को
याद करती जा।

कोई ग़म नहीं,
कोई शिकायत नहीं।
आने वाला है वो पल,
जिसका शायद इंतज़ार था कभी।

आंखों में ख्वाब थे ज़रूर,
आशाएं उड़ान भर चुकी थी हुज़ूर।
चट्टानों से कभी डरे नही,
तूफानों के संभाले हैं हमने फितूर।

ले गए तुम हमारे पंख,
लेकिन सपने छोड़ गए।
ले गए वो रथ,
लेकिन ताज छोड़ गए।

उठेंगे हम वो ही सूरज देख कर,
फिर करना है शुक्रिया तुमको देखकर।
फिर से मुस्कुराएंगे ज़रूर,
सिर पर वो ही ताज पहनकर।

Love Unknown

When life is going so perfect,
And it's all going so well.
A sudden noise wakes me up,
Says, don't dream, it's a long wait.

And then I wait and wait,
Wait to be loved again.
Heard again smile again,
Just wait to dream again.

Each day a new promise,
Each day a new day.
With new hopes the sun sets,
I see, I see everything fades away.

I give my heart,
I give my soul.
I give my body,
For the love unknown.

It hurts and I am in pain,
I feel weak in love.
What more could I do to make our dream come
true,
Please explain.

When time stops and I will be gone,
Someone tell him what he meant to me.
Tell him I was tired, tell him I was in pain,
For my life I tried and I failed forever again.

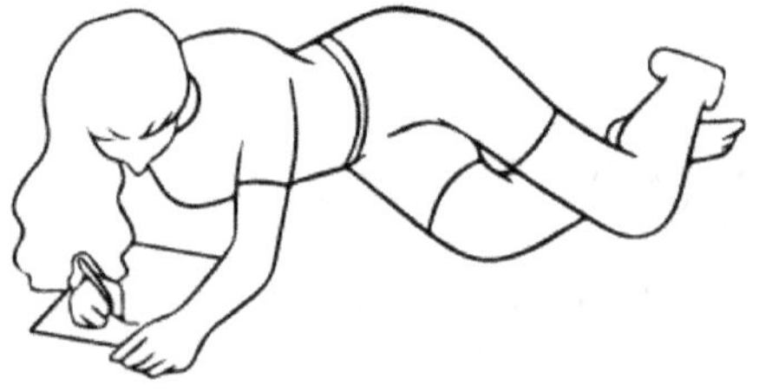

My City of Dreams

I live on the Land of Hopes,
I live in the world of Dreams.
Here I see myself growing,
Oh! A paradise it seems.

I want to reach the sky,
I want to light every street I pass by.
I want to do all that I wish to,
Please, don't ask me why.

Cool breeze touches me,
Makes me feel so strong.
Heat of the Sun,
Gives me the whole world's warmth.

Such a lovely place,
Such peaceful air.
I want my people around,
Just my happiness to share.

I can't ask for more,
From the city that never sleeps.
From the city that smiles and dreams,
From the city that believes and gives.

Untill—

A sudden shake I felt,
A loud noise I heard.
Crowded streets,
But alone everyone was here.

So painful to see,
Blood flowing around me.
Terror entered in here,
And the city is full of fear.

How terrible it feels,
Today, I have nothing to give.
Just when I realized,
Reality is killing my dreams.

Just Live

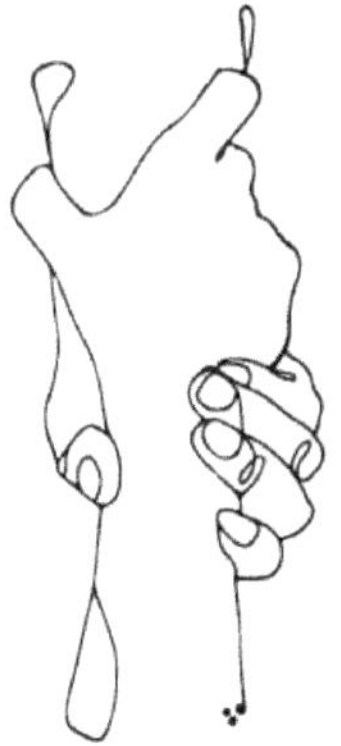

Don't be a star,
And shine for your own.
But be a light and give them more.

Don't be a sound,
That destroys all around.
But be the music—music of love,
And pass to the thousands of smiles you have
known.

Don't just be a man,
For life will end it all.
Be a human being,
And live long.

Don't be a solitaire,
Proud to be.
Hold my hands, come hold my hands,
Let's form a ring, between you and me.

Don't cry—when you have it all.

Pick up a dream,
You have always seen.
Pick up a hope,
You have always known.

Pick up that love,
You have always got.
Pick up those colours,
You have always drawn.

Pick up the beauty,
You have always felt.
Pick up that peace,
You always get

And 'Just Live.'

That's The Way It Is

Oh! My love,
I have to say.
When I first met you,
On a sunny day.

Your eyes were bright,
And staring at me.
They said it all.
For you and for me.

I had no clue what to do.
But you made sure
Without any fear
You said to me, "Yes my love, my love is true."

I looked at you,
With a smile.
And you promised to me
You said, "Just chill, everything will be fine."

We exchanged our vows,
And tied a knot.
On that special day, you sang a song,
I can't forget, your voice echoes in my heart.

Everything seems so beautiful,
With my lucky charm around me.
I felt so protected,
With my perfect man around me.

But now things have changed,
With the time and with the days.
I search for my love,
In many different ways.

I know it's true,
When it's me and you.
But it hurts to say—Darling, it's so unfair,
When it seems you just don't care.

I have lost that charm,
I have lost that smile.
Oh! My love, why can't you notice,
When you look into my eyes.

I know it's different,
And it really is.
But I just smile and say,
Maybe, 'That's The Way It Is.'

क्या हो तुम

कुछ अपना सा
कुछ सपना सा हो तुम
अजीब हो
पर दिल के करीब हो तुम
हंसी की वजह कभी
तो कभी आंसुओं की तकलीफ़ हो तुम
अजीब हो
पर दिल के करीब हो तुम
प्यार करना सिखाते भी
प्यार निभाना दिखाते भी
अजीब हो
पर दिल के करीब हो तुम
कभी बच्चे जैसे रूठे
कभी समझदारी से मुझे मानते
सच यार
अजीब हो
पर दिल के करीब हो तुम

इश्क़ का रंग

इन दिनों हाल है कुछ ऐसा,
हर जगह तुम्हारा एहसास है ये कैसा।
खामोशियों को कभी सुनना हुज़ूर,
तुम्हारा नाम वो अक्सर लेती है हुज़ूर।

मेरी ज़िंदगी मे,
तुम्हारी जगह बनाते-बनाते
तुम खुद मेरी ज़िंदगी बन गए
ये राज़ किसको हम बताते।

खुदा से सच्चा प्यार था मांगा,
रूह तक बसे ऐसा एहसास था मांगा।
दस्तक जब दी तुमने,
क्या थी खबर खुदा वो सब खुद ही ले आता।

अक्सर पूछते हैं लोग,
ये नूर किसका है चढ़ा।
नाम ज़ुबान पे नहीं ले पाती,
लेकिन आखों मे उन्होंने तुमको ही है पढ़ा।

तुमरे इश्क का रंग,
कुछ इस तरह चढ़ा।
हर रंग मुझपर,
तुम जैसा दिखा।

अब जो भी हो ऐ मोहब्बत,
सपनों की दुनिया से निकलकर
अपनी दुनिया बनाएँ चल,
घर एक अपना, एक मंदिर सजा लें चल।

हाथ थाम लेना,
लकीरें मिला देना ।
खुदा तू मेरा,
मुझको तुमसे कभी जुदा ना होने देना।

ज़िंदगी एक खेल

समझ गए तुम्हे ऐ ज़िंदगी,
मुस्कुराने की दी है वजह कई।
एक मोड़ तुमने बनाया,
जब राह खो गई।

तुमने आंसू भी दिए,
और गम भी।
तुमने हौसला भी दिया,
और उम्मीद भी।

कभी अकेलेपन का एहसास
कभी कोई अपना अपने पास।
कभी वही पुरानी बात,
कभी कुछ बहुत खास।

महसूस किया जो तुमने दिखाया,
गिला शिकवा भी बहुत किया।
आज माना तुम्हें,
क्या ग़ज़ब का खेल है खेला।

जो चीज़ बनी अपनी,
वह ना बनी अपने दिल की।
जो दिल से लगाई,
उसे कभी अपने पास न रखने दी।

कुछ उलझनों मे डाल ही देती ऐ ज़िंदगी,
डर नहीं अब तेरे फैसलों का।
हमने देखा है किसी की आँखों में,
रिश्तों को कैसे है निभाना।

We Are Caged

Today we are caged,
In our own thoughts.
We are caged,
In the terror, we ourselves have got.
Today we are caged,
In our own fears.
We are caged,
In our own tears.
They said freedom is life,
And we lived up to it.
Killing, destroying and misusing,
Who said it was right?
We are now caged,
With what we made alive.
We are now caged,
And dying each day to survive.
For all the years we lost,
To create that existed.
We realized at this time,
It's all gone and dusted.
For all those who thought,
I am the King and I am the Queen.
I am the owner of my own kin
For all those who thought,
Money brought me happiness,

And only my life is priceless.
Dear Sir and Ma'am,
Life has turned the page,
And today we all are caged.
Well! Well!
We have not made it that bad,
At least, we gave animals and birds their share…

एक अनमोल चीज़

एक अनमोल चीज़ पाई है,
तुमसे बिछड़ कर।
साथ दिया है हर वक्त,
मेरे साथ रहकर।

अकेले मे,
बस उसी को देखा।
सहारा बनकर,
बस चले आते हैं साथ में।

तुम्हे खोकर देखो,
कितनी धनवान हो गई हूं।
इस पागलपन मे तो,
पलके झपकाना ही भूल गई हूं।

यह मत सोचो,
कि भूल गए हैं तुम्हें।
आखिर यही तो चीज़,
तुमसे मिली है हमें।

रोज़ बातें करती हूँ,
इस अनमोल चीज़ से।
तुम्हारी याद मे,
बहते हैं जब ये आँसू इन आँखों से।

तुम्हारी बेटी

एक उम्र गुज़र गई,
ये सोचते-सोचते।
अगर प्यार था इतना,
तो जाने क्यूँ देते ।

बचपन में जब,
हाथ छुड़ाकर हम भागते।
तो क्यो संभालने,
तुम्हारे हाथ आगे बढ़ते।

हमारी यादों को,
तस्वीरों में उतारा ।
कभी कुछ ना कहते तुम,
बस तुम्हारा दिल भर आता।

सब कुछ लुटाकर ,
प्यार निभाना सिखाया।
खुद कम जिए,
लेकिन हमे जीना सिखाया।

कहा था तुमने खूब,
खुश रहना जहा भी रहो तुम।
मगर आंसुओं को पीकर,
खुद जीते रहे तुम।

कितना भी छुपाओ,
समझते है सब हम।
रोकना चाहते थे तुम,
साथ में जब दिन थे कम।

जब कदम नई दुनिया की ओर बढ़े,
रोक ही लेते तुम।
सदा के लिए ना सही,
कुछ दिन और ही रह लेते हम।

चलो अब ज़िंदगी नई रिश्ते नए,
लो नाम भी बदल लिया हमने।
तुम्हारी बेटी ही रहूंगी सदा,
ये खून ने समझा दिया हमें।

Darling Sister

If I had a Genie,
And a wish to make.
I would ask,
For my childhood again.

I would keep you by my side,
And let you be my guide.
I would fight and cry,
But still look for you from the corner of my eye.

I would get that kitchen set out,
In the hope, this time you won't shout.
I would hope you leave that video game,
And not feel my toys are lame.

I would still follow you everywhere,
And do what you dare.
I would still be myself,
And admire you with a stare.

I would promise,
Not to irritate you with my girly talks.
I would wear your shorts,
And give up on my frocks.

Once again,
We would cut the same cake.
You are the youngest,
You would love to fake.

It was easy,
To grow up with you, dear Sis.
As you walked the thorns before me,
And gave me a sigh of bliss.

I wish to rewind and relive,
Those years we laughed and cherished.
When together felt like forever,
When staying apart was never the fear.

As we grew,
I looked up to you.
You made me believe,
Guardian Angels exist and they were true.

I can't thank you enough,
And I don't have words to say.
But I feel a part of me,
Is going miles away.

But I am so happy,
As now is the time.
She found her perfect man,
She says that with a broad smile.

My angel is blushing,
And looking so fine.
Her dream is coming true,
Oh! It happens to very few.

Dear Genie,
Now listen to me.
Make my one wish come true,
Let all my sister's wishes be fulfilled.
As they are very few.
She is simple and sweet,
Bless her always
'Cause that's all she needs,
Her love and her space.
Keep her happy and content,
As she will not ask for more than this
She is strong but she forgets
She lives for others

She is so selfless.
If you think I asked a lot
Remember—
She deserved more than you thought.

Mother's Love

I don't remember
The darkest days of my life
I don't remember
My first sunlight
I don't know when I first grew in you
I don't know
When I was ready to first see you
I might have kicked you
I might have pushed you
I might have tickled you
Or
I might have behaved the best
Among the rest
But today—
I want to thank you, Mom
For keeping me safe
Even in the darkest days of my life
For showing me my first sunlight
I am so happy mom
Everyday, I grew up in your arm
I know I am not the first one
But being the youngest is more fun
Thank you, Mom
For being my friend
For your love

Which has no end.
Thank you, Mom
For bringing me up in the best way
For all that you had you gave away.
I love you forever
And I pray to God
In my next life
I want you as my Mom.

बेटियां किसकी होती हैं?

बेटियां किसकी होती हैं
जहाँ पैदा होती हैं
वहाँ से भी पराई हो जाती हैं
तो बिटिया किसकी होती है

घर लक्ष्मी आई ये कहते हैं
बड़े प्यार और लाड़ से संभालते हैं
जब दुनिया की जंग वो अकेले लड़ती है
तब ये बिटिया किसकी होती है

जिस भाई की कलाई पर
जो हर साल राखी बांधती है
वो वक्त आने पर "मुसीबतों का सामना खुद कर" ये
कह जाता है
तो बिटिया किसकी होती है

शादी तो धूम धाम से करते हैं
एक पराए घर से होकर
दूसरे पराए घर ही तो जाती है
ये बिटिया किसकी होती है

पति, बच्चे, सास, ससुर
सबको तो संभालती है
पर वक्त आने पर किसी को उसको समझना पड़े
तो खुद से बातें करती है और खुद को ही संभालती है

वो आती तो है इस दुनिया में किसी के घर
पर वो खुद का घर कहाँ बना पाती है
वो सिर्फ मेहनत करती है
और पराए घर मे सिर्फ खुशियां लाती है

रात को जब
वो अकेले ही रोती है
वो सबसे दूर खुद से ही रहती है और कहती है
ये बिटिया आखिर किसकी होती है?

मुझको "मैं" रहने दो

मुझको "मैं" रहने दो
अगर हवा के जैसे उड़ना चाहूँ
तो मुझको उड़ने दो
अगर पर्वत के जैसे ठहरना चाहूँ
तो ठहरने दो
मुझको "मैं" रहने दो
मुझको तुम्हारी सोच ना बनाओ
मैं जैसी बनी हूं
मुझको तुम वैसे ही अपनाओ
मुझको "मैं" रहने दो
ना बनाओ मुझको
लक्ष्मी, सरस्वती या दुर्गा
और न बनाओ
कोई हूर, हसीना या अप्सरा
मुझको बस "मैं" ही रहने दो
मैं तुम जैसी नहीं

मैं किसी और के जैसी भी नहीं
हां हूं मैं अलग
क्योंकि मुझ जैसी मैं एक ही बनी
मत रखो कोई नाम
जो मेरी पहचान बदल दे
बदलो तुम्हारी सोच
जिसको हम इंसानियत का नाम दे
नहीं बनना किसी की उम्मीद मुझे
नहीं संभालना हर किसी को हर वक्त मुझे
नहीं सीखना सब कुछ मुझे
नहीं करना कोई संघर्ष मुझे
ये तो सच है जान गई हूं अब
नाम दिए गए कई अच्छा कह कर
बेटी, बहन, बहू, या मां
सबको जवाब देना है यह
क्योंकि—
बेटी अच्छी तब तक
जब तक वो बोलना ना सीख जाए
बहन अच्छी तब तक
जब तक वो अपनी मर्ज़ी ना चलाए
प्रेमिका अच्छी तब तक
जब तक वो "नहीं" कहना न सीख जाए
बहू अच्छी तब तक
जब तक बेटा खुश रहे
बीवी अच्छी तब तक
जब तक वो टूट ना जाए
और मां—
मां अच्छी तब तक
जब तक वो सहना जाने